STAR WARS

THE FORCE AWAKENS
NEW ADVENTURES

Written by David Fentiman

Written and Edited by David Fentiman
Project Art Editor Owen Bennett
Creative Technical Support Tom Morse
Senior Pre-Production Producer Jennifer Murray
Senior Producer Alex Bell
Managing Editor Sadie Smith
Managing Art Editor Ron Stobbart
Art Director Lisa Lanzarini
Publisher Julie Ferris
Publishing Director Simon Beecroft

For Cameron + Company
Designers Dagmar Trojanek, Amy Wheless, and Jillian Lungaro
Creative Director Iain Morris

For Lucasfilm
Executive Editor Jonathan W. Rinzler
Image Archives Stacey Leong
Art Director Troy Alders
Story Group Leland Chee, Pablo Hidalgo, and Rayne Roberts

First American Edition, 2015
Published in the United States by DK Publishing
345 Hudson Street, New York, New York 10014

Page design copyright © 2015 Dorling Kindersley Limited
A Penguin Random House Company
15 16 17 18 19 10 9 8 7 6 5 4 3 2 1
001–195846–December/2015

© & TM 2015 LUCASFILM LTD.

A catalog record for this book is available from the Library of Congress.

ISBN 978-1-4654-3813-3 (Hardback)
ISBN 978-1-4654-3814-0 (Paperback)

DK books are available at special discounts when purchased in bulk for sales promotions,
premiums, fund-raising, or educational use. For details, contact: DK Publishing Special
Markets, 345 Hudson Street, New York, New York 10014
SpecialSales@dk.com

Printed and bound in the USA

A WORLD OF IDEAS:
SEE ALL THERE IS TO KNOW

www.dk.com
www.starwars.com

Contents

A NEW BATTLE

The galaxy is in danger!
The evil First Order wants to take over.
Only the Resistance can stop it.

THE RESISTANCE

The brave Resistance fights against the First Order.
General Leia is the leader of the Resistance. She has
many pilots and soldiers to help her. The Resistance
has a secret base on a planet named D'Qar.

THE FIRST ORDER

The First Order is all that remains of the Empire.
The evil Empire once ruled the galaxy. It was
destroyed many years ago by Leia and her
brother, Luke. Now the First Order wants revenge!

Kylo Ren

Kylo Ren is the First Order's
greatest warrior. He is very
powerful, and very evil. Kylo uses
a weapon known as a lightsaber.
He also uses the Force. This is
a strange energy that gives him
special powers!

General Leia

General Leia is also a princess. Many years ago, she fought against the Empire with her brother, Luke. He was a noble warrior known as a Jedi. Luke disappeared a long time ago, and now Leia is trying to find him.

C-3PO and R2-D2

R2-D2 and C-3PO are old friends of Leia's. They are both droids. C-3PO serves Leia in the Resistance, but R2-D2 has been shut down for a long time. Ever since his master Luke Skywalker went away, R2 has not spoken to anyone.

Poe Dameron

Poe is General Leia's best pilot. His ship is called an X-wing. Poe flies his X-wing with great skill. Leia sends Poe on a secret mission to help find her brother, Luke. Poe is very brave and would do anything for Leia.

POE'S MISSION

MISSION GOAL 1

Fly to desert planet
named Jakku

MISSION GOAL 2

Meet with the explorer
Lor San Tekka

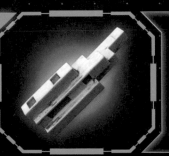

MISSION GOAL 3

Get secret artifact
from Lor and bring
it back to Leia

MISSION PLANET Jakku

POSSIBLE DANGERS

- First Order might attack at any time
- Jakku has savage wildlife and dangerous deserts

Finn

Finn was once a stormtrooper. Stormtroopers are the First Order's soldiers. His real name is FN-2187, but his friends call him Finn. Finn sees how evil the First Order is, and he decides to run away.

Rey

Rey comes from the planet Jakku. She works in a junkyard, and never expects to join the Resistance. Rey is an expert at fixing machines. She has built a speeder out of spare parts. Rey slowly realizes that she can use the Force.

BB-8

BB-8 is a type of robot called an astromech droid. He helps Poe pilot his X-wing. BB-8 is an unusual droid. His whole body rolls when he moves, but his head stays still! BB-8 is very loyal to Poe.

THE FIRST ORDER

The Resistance is our enemy. With your help, we will destroy it and rule the galaxy. It is up to you, brave stormtroopers!

BE FEARLESS

FOLLOW ORDERS

TRUST YOUR LEADERS

Captain Phasma

Captain Phasma leads the First Order's stormtroopers. She wears special silver armor and is very frightening. The only thing she cares about is destroying the First Order's enemies.

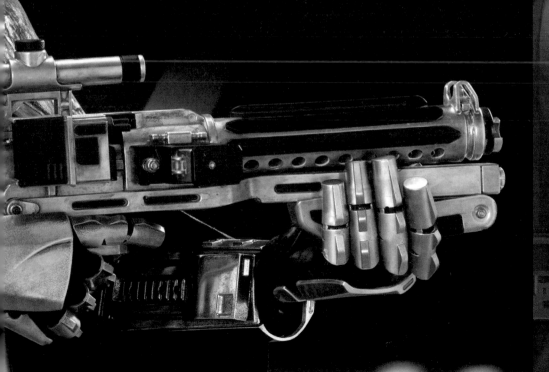

General Hux

General Hux is in charge of the
First Order's army and fleet of
starships. Hux has built a huge
weapon named the Starkiller.
He wants to use it to defeat
the Resistance.

THE STARKILLER

The Starkiller is a giant weapon. It takes up
a whole planet! It can smash an entire star
system with a single blast. The Starkiller
is guarded by thousands of stormtroopers.

ADVANTAGES	DISADVANTAGES
► Able to destroy an entire star system ► Shields are very strong ► Has very powerful defenses	► Cannot move ► Cannot be hidden ► If damaged, may destroy itself ► Takes time to charge up

The Resistance Base

The Resistance base is hidden
on a planet named D'Qar.
The base is where the Resistance
keeps its starships.

The Resistance base also has a command center. It is buried deep underground. This is where General Leia and her officers plan their battles.

Admiral Statura

Admiral Statura is General Leia's second-in-command at the Resistance base. He helps Leia plan missions against the First Order. Admiral Statura is very smart. He knows a lot about weapons and vehicles.

Han Solo and Chewbacca

Han was once a smuggler, but he helped Leia defeat the Empire. He and his copilot Chewbacca have been together for a very long time. Their ship is called the *Millennium Falcon*. Han cares for Leia, and he agrees to join the Resistance.

Admiral Ackbar

Admiral Ackbar is one of Leia's officers. He is a Mon Calamari.

He fought beside Leia in the war against the Empire, 30 years ago. They have been through many dangerous battles together. Leia trusts Ackbar with her life.

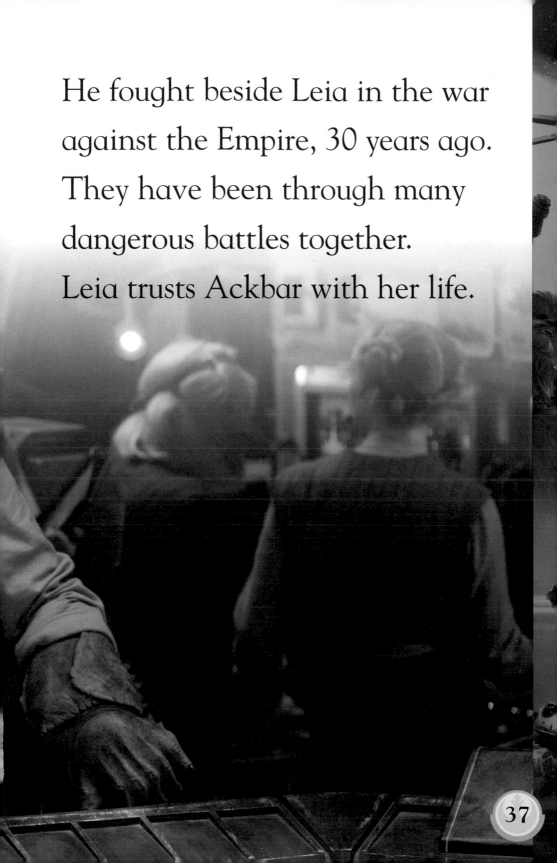

PILOT PROFILE
Poe Dameron

RANK: **Commander**

HOMEWORLD: **Yavin 4**

SKILL: **Improvising**

PILOT PROFILE
Snap Wexley

RANK: **Captain**

HOMEWORLD: **Akiva**

SKILL: **Scouting missions**

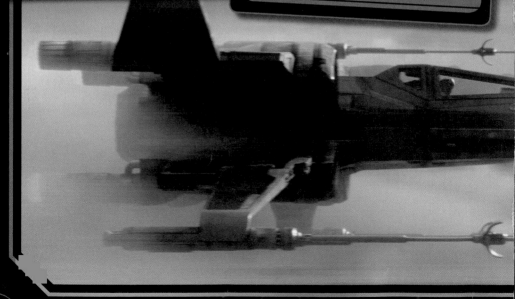

PILOT PROFILE
Jess Pava

RANK: **Lieutenant**

HOMEWORLD: **Dandoran**

SKILL: **Ship-to-ship combat**

PILOT PROFILE
Nien Nunb

RANK: **Lieutenant Commander**

HOMEWORLD: **Sullust**

SKILL: **Navigation**

X WINGS

Astromech droid

Laser cannon

Cockpit

Nose cone

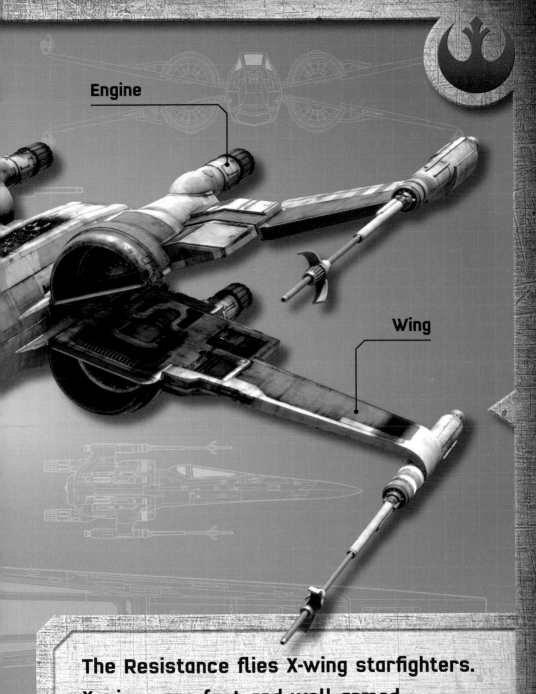

Engine

Wing

The Resistance flies X-wing starfighters.
X-wings are fast and well armed.
The X-wing pilots must try to
destroy the Starkiller!

Quiz

1. Who is the First Order's greatest warrior?

2. Who leads the Resistance?

3. What is the First Order's giant weapon called?

4. What type of droid is BB-8?

5. What kind of starfighters does the Resistance use?

Answers on page 45

Glossary

Droid A robot

The Empire An evil group that once ruled the galaxy

The First Order A powerful army created from the remains of the Empire

The Force A strange and powerful energy that has a light side and a dark side

General Someone who leads soldiers in battle

Jedi Someone who uses the light side of the Force to do good

The Resistance A group that defends the galaxy from the First Order

Smuggler Someone who transports illegal goods

Index

Answers to the quiz on pages 42 and 43:
1. Kylo Ren 2. General Leia 3. The Starkiller
4. An astromech droid 5. X-wings

Guide for Parents

DK Readers is a four-level interactive reading adventure series for children, developing the habit of reading widely for both pleasure and information. These books have an exciting main narrative interspersed with a range of reading genres to suit your child's reading ability, as required by the Common Core State Standards. Each book is designed to develop your child's reading skills, fluency, grammar awareness, and comprehension in order to build confidence and engagement when reading.

Ready for a *Beginning to Read* book
YOUR CHILD SHOULD

- be familiar with using beginning letter sounds and context clues to figure out unfamiliar words.
- be aware of the need for a slight pause at commas and a longer one at periods.
- alter his/her expression for questions and exclamations.

A Valuable and Shared Reading Experience

For many children, reading requires much effort, but adult participation can make this both fun and easier. So here are a few tips on how to use this book with your child.

TIP 1 Check out the contents together before your child begins:

- read the text about the book on the back cover.
- flip through the book and stop to chat about the contents page together to heighten your child's interest and expectation.
- make use of unfamiliar or difficult words on the page in a brief discussion.
- chat about the non-fiction reading features used in the book, such as headings, captions, recipes, lists or charts.

TIP 2 Support your child as he/she reads the story pages:

- Give the book to your child to read and turn the pages.

- where necessary, encourage your child to break a word into syllables, sound out each one, and then flow the syllables together. Ask him/her to reread the sentence to check the meaning.

- when there's a question mark or an exclamation mark, encourage your child to vary his/her voice as he/she reads the sentence. Demonstrate how to do this if it is helpful.

TIP 3 Chat at the end of each page:

- the factual pages tend to be more difficult than the story pages, and are designed to be shared with your child.

- ask questions about the text and the meaning of the words used. These help to develop comprehension skills and awareness of the language used.

A FEW ADDITIONAL TIPS

- Always encourage your child to try reading difficult words by themselves. Praise any self-corrections, for example, "I like the way you sounded out that word and then changed the way you said it, to make sense."

- Try to read together everyday. Reading little and often is best. These books are divided into manageable chapters for one reading session. However, after 10 minutes, only keep going if your child wants to read on.

- Read other books of different types to your child just for enjoyment and information.

Have you read these other great books from DK?

BEGINNING TO READ

Meet some brave heroes. Who do you think saved the galaxy?

Join Luke Skywalker and his friends on their adventures.

Visit a construction site and watch the mega machines in action.

BEGINNING TO READ ALONE

 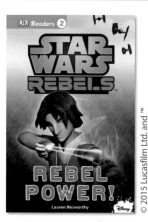 

Meet a band of rebels, brave enough to take on the Empire!

Go on another adventure with the rebels of Lothal!

Discover Jupiter with its colorful clouds and awesome moons.